illustrated by : Jade Mempin

1

Table of Contents

Introduction...4

Jake's Exciting Project 6

A New Friend, a New Way 12

The Power of Kindness 20

Courage on the Court..............................26

The Power of Being You.......................... 32

Dive Beyond Fear......................................40

Wings of Appreciation.............................48

Oliver's Tasty Adventure...........................54

A Symphony of Stars................................ 60

The Pumpkin King 66

Introduction

Hello, extraordinary boy!

In these stories, you'll meet regular boys who faced challenges just like you. They didn't have superpowers or fancy gadgets, but they had something even more important: courage.

Life can throw curveballs, and sometimes you might doubt yourself. It happens to the best of us. But what you're about to discover in these stories is that doubt can be defeated, fears can be conquered, and dreams can become your reality.

Here's the secret: You're never alone in this journey called life. The characters in these stories, and so many others out there, have walked a similar path.

They've faced struggles, climbed mountains, and turned their dreams into accomplishments.

Now, it's your turn. These stories are like roadmaps, guiding you on a journey of self-discovery, self-confidence, and unwavering self-esteem.

Believe in yourself, just as we believe in you. You've got what it takes to tackle any challenge, bounce back from setbacks, and achieve greatness. You're more extraordinary than you know.

So, as you flip through these pages and dive into the first story, remember this: Your journey to becoming the hero of your own inspiring story starts right here, right now. You're ready. Your time is here. Let's begin this incredible adventure together!

Jake's Exciting Project

Have you ever felt excited about taking on a new challenge? Some adventures can be thrilling, and you might wonder how you'll ever manage them. Do you put your heart and soul into achieving your goals?

How much effort are you willing to invest, and how does it make you feel when you finally accomplish them? Don't worry, young adventurer, your enthusiasm is a sign that you care, and when you work hard, you uncover incredible experiences. When you learn from those experiences, you create lasting memories.

Jake burst through the front door one day, his face beaming with excitement. He tossed his backpack onto the floor and rushed to find his dad. "Dad! You won't believe this! I have an amazing opportunity for a school project. It's going to be a real adventure!" Jake's dad grinned, knowing that his son always thrived on new challenges and exciting tasks.

"Tell me all about it," his dad encouraged.

Jake couldn't contain his enthusiasm. "I have to plan and execute a treasure hunt for my class, and it's due by the end of the week.

Jake was filled with excitement, but there was a hint of nervousness as well because he had never organized anything like this before. The most adventurous thing he had done was a scavenger hunt in his own backyard.

"Did your teacher give you guidelines for the project?" his dad asked.

"Yes!" Jake replied, retrieving the project guidelines from his backpack. His dad motioned for him to sit down, reminding him to take a deep breath and calm down. "And remember, no running in the house," he added with a smile.

Jake nodded, taking a deep breath. As he reviewed the instructions, he realized there were many ways to plan a treasure hunt. After some thought, he decided on a pirate-themed treasure hunt that would take place in their local park.

His dad, seeing Jake's determination, suggested, "Why don't you start by making a list of items and supplies you'll need?"

Jake agreed and began jotting down a list of materials: a treasure chest, pirate hats, maps, clues, and some small prizes for the participants.

That evening, after finishing his homework and having dinner with his family, Jake and his dad went to the store to gather all the necessary items. As they wandered through the store, Jake carefully checked off each item on his list. It was tempting to grab more exciting items, but he knew he needed to stay focused.

There were so many interesting things in the store, but he remained determined.

Back home, Jake laid out all the supplies. There was a lot to do, and he felt a bit overwhelmed.

He worried that he might not be able to plan a thrilling treasure hunt in time, or that it wouldn't be as exciting as he imagined. He didn't know where to start.

Remembering his dad's advice, Jake closed his eyes, took a deep breath, and exhaled slowly. He decided to begin by creating a detailed treasure map. Once he had a plan in place, everything seemed more manageable. If he worked diligently, he would have plenty of time to organize the hunt.

Jake worked tirelessly for the rest of the week, experiencing occasional moments of nervousness. But each time doubt crept in, he took a deep breath and reminded himself that he could do it. When he looked at his completed treasure hunt on the due date, he still felt a hint of uncertainty.

However, when his classmates participated and expressed their excitement, he realized he had succeeded in creating an unforgettable adventure.

Jake and his dad left the treasure hunt in the park, and as they walked away, Jake felt a sense of pride for tackling the challenge and turning it into an exciting adventure. He learned that even when doubts and nerves tried to hold him back, with a deep breath and a well-thought-out plan, he could accomplish great things because he was a determined and resourceful young boy.

So, what do you think? Do you believe that no matter the challenge, you have the ability to take on exciting adventures? Even when you have doubts, remember to take a deep breath, make a plan, and have confidence in yourself, because with determination and a bit of help, you can accomplish anything you set your mind to!

A New Friend, a New Way

Do you like having fun with your friends and feeling happy? Your friends think you're special because you're kind, funny, and brave. But what if you have a really bad day, and your friends can't cheer you up?

Can meeting a new friend who sees things differently change your day? Let's see how it happened to a boy named Liam. Liam had lots of friends, but could they help him on a tough day? Maybe a new friend, with a special way of looking at things, could make a difference.

Liam loved spending time with his friends after school. Whenever the weather was fair, he'd join his parents at the community playground, where he'd meet up with a few of his pals. They'd run around, playing imaginative games like camping, cooking, and going on thrilling adventures. Using his imagination was one of Liam's favorite things to do, and his friends always eagerly embraced the imaginative stories he spun.

One day, while they were engrossed in their play, the weather suddenly turned. Rain began to pour, forcing all the parents and children to scatter back to their homes. Liam was a bit disheartened because they hadn't finished their story, and it seemed unlikely they ever would.

As they walked back to the car, Liam slipped on a wet patch of cement, resulting in a scrape on his knee that bled a little. The sight of his own blood made him cry, although the pain wasn't all that bad. When they arrived home, his dad cleaned and bandaged the scrape. Liam started feeling a bit silly for shedding tears over something so trivial.

At dinner, Liam couldn't wait to eat. Ignoring his mom's warning about the piping-hot mashed potatoes, he eagerly took a big spoonful, burning his tongue in the process. By the end of the night, he'd bumped his head, scraped his elbow, dropped and shattered a plate, suffered a paper cut while reading his book, and couldn't find his beloved stuffed lion that he usually slept with. So many things went wrong in a short span, leaving him feeling very grumpy.

"Well," his mom said while gently stroking Liam's hair, "hopefully, you'll sleep it off and wake up feeling better."

However, that wasn't the case. When Liam woke up the next day, he felt even grumpier, and for some reason, he was even more tired. Although his family tried to engage him in conversation during breakfast, Liam barely mumbled any responses. On the bus, when his friend Ben sat down next to him and asked how he was doing, Liam grumbled that he was "fine" but "didn't feel like talking this morning."

As he walked down the school hallway, his friends waved at him, and the teachers greeted him with a cheerful "good morning." But Liam wasn't interested in any of it. They couldn't possibly know about his terrible night, and he had no intention of discussing it with them. He was tired, sore, and his tongue still hurt from the scalding mashed potatoes. He figured he might as well embrace the grumpy mood since nothing seemed to be going his way.

When class began, Liam suddenly realized he'd forgotten to use the bathroom and requested the hall pass.

Though he could sense a hint of annoyance in the teacher's response, she granted his request, saying, "Be back soon." It wasn't as if he'd forgotten on purpose!

As he walked down the hallway, Liam noticed a boy using metal crutches to walk towards the boys' restroom. A grown-up accompanied him, and they entered the bathroom together. Liam thought to himself, "I'd hate to have to go to the toilet with a grown-up." He'd never seen that boy before, but his school was quite large, so he assumed he wouldn't see him again.

However, he was wrong. During lunch, Liam saw the same boy again. The adult with him helped carry his lunch tray, but the boy sat down by himself. Liam watched as the boy struggled to open his applesauce, causing it to spill all over him. Yet, the boy simply laughed, shook his head, and wiped the sauce off his shirt. Then, Liam saw him accidentally drop a fork on the floor. Although the grown-up picked it up and fetched him a new one, the boy didn't appear the least bit frustrated. He noticed Liam watching him and waved.

Feeling a bit embarrassed but intrigued by the boy, Liam waved back. After lunch, he approached the boy and asked, "Hey, are you new here?"

"Yeah," the boy replied with a warm smile, "I started last week, but the teachers had to get me situated. I'm Tom."

"Hello, Tom. I'm Liam," Liam introduced himself. "Do you want some help with your bookbag?"

"Nope, I've got it," Tom replied, shrugging the bookbag onto his shoulders in an awkward manner. Oddly enough, he didn't seem bothered by it at all. "It helps me get stronger," Tom added, grinning, revealing two missing front teeth.

Despite his grumpy mood, Liam couldn't help but smile back at Tom. "Are you heading to recess?" Liam asked.

"Yes, but I can only walk around," Tom explained. "I can't run, jump, or do cartwheels."

Liam chuckled and shook his head. "How can you be so happy?" he asked. "You always have a grown-up with you, you spilled applesauce on your shirt, dropped your fork, and ate lunch by yourself... Doesn't that make you grumpy?"

Tom laughed heartily. "Ha! Nope!" he said. "If I got upset every time something went wrong, I'd never be happy. It's better to have a good time when things get messed up instead of letting it get to me."

This perspective struck Liam profoundly. He had never considered looking at his own blunders as something humorous or an opportunity for enjoyment. He usually just became grumpy because he felt he had done something wrong.

"That's such a different way to think!" Liam exclaimed.

Tom nodded. "Yep, it's not always easy, but my hands and legs don't work as well as other people's do. Instead of being angry about it, I accept that I'm going to drop things, run into things, and have my grown-up around to help. You know, everyone makes mistakes and gets clumsy sometimes anyway. I just might do it a little more than others."

Liam was amazed. "Wow, that's a great way to think!" he said, suddenly realizing that he didn't have to be grumpy all the time. From that day forward, he and Tom walked around the playground during recess, making new friends and sharing laughs. Liam started to view his own stumbles and fumbles in a different light, always searching for the humor in them. Whenever he found himself slipping into a grumpy mood, he remembered Tom's positive outlook on life, and it brought a smile to his face.

The Power of Kindness

Have you ever encountered someone who seemed very different from you? What did you think about them? Did you realize that despite the differences, you might have more in common than you thought? It's essential to remember that appearances can be deceiving, and it's what's inside a person that truly matters. You never know who someone truly is until you get to know them.

Meet Daniel, a boy who loved the changing seasons, especially the transition from summer to fall. The vibrant colors of the leaves and the crisp autumn air always filled him with joy. One day, while walking to school, Daniel heard a group of rowdy boys causing a commotion. Curiosity got the best of him, and he approached the group.

"What are you guys up to? It sounds like you're being mean to someone," Daniel said, concerned. He had witnessed these boys bothering others before, and he didn't want it to happen again.

As the circle of boys parted, Daniel saw that they were bullying a smaller boy named Max. Daniel shook his head in disappointment. "I can't believe you would pick on someone smaller and younger than you," he scolded.

Max, the boy in the center, was notably smaller than the others. His face displayed a mix of anger and frustration. "I'm not younger than them. I'm in the same grade!" he retorted, wiping away tears. He turned away from Daniel and the bullies and walked off in a huff.

Feeling empathy for Max, Daniel realized that he was in the same grade as him, not younger as he had assumed. He regretted his initial judgment and followed Max. "Hey!" Daniel called out, catching up to him. "You're new here, right? I'm Daniel."

Max walked briskly, and Daniel had to hurry to keep up. "Wow, you're a fast walker," Daniel remarked.

Max stopped abruptly and looked at Daniel, his face still etched with anger. "What do you want?" he snapped.

"I'm sorry I thought you were younger," Daniel apologized. "I couldn't tell with all those guys crowding around you."

Max looked surprised. "Oh," he said, "I thought you were going to make fun of me."

"Why would I do that?" Daniel asked. "Just because you're small doesn't define who you are. Our bodies grow differently, and they change every day. It's what's inside that counts." Daniel pointed to his heart and his head. "What's your name?"

Max blinked as if he had never heard such words before. "I'm Max. Yes, I'm new here," he replied, exhaling. "Thanks for stepping in with those guys. They were pretty mean."

Daniel acknowledged, "Sadly, they can be like that sometimes. Maybe they're just bored or don't know how to interact with others."

Max nodded in agreement. "Wow, you're really understanding."

"No, what they did to you or anyone else isn't okay!" Daniel declared. However, he wanted to shift the conversation away from bullies.

Instead, he was curious about Max and his background. "So, where did you live before?"

As Daniel and Max continued talking, they reached the school. They sat together during lunch, sharing laughter and stories. Daniel discovered that Max's entire family was short, but he was exceptionally fast and had a great sense of humor. This impressed Daniel the most because it meant Max made up his own jokes, making him exceptionally funny.

Daniel and Max formed a strong friendship, and Daniel invited Max over to his house. Max's jokes even made Daniel's parents laugh, bringing happiness to the whole family.

One day, during recess, the group of rowdy boys challenged the other kids to a race. Daniel knew they were doing it to make fun of those who couldn't finish quickly, but Max wanted to prove how fast he was. Max stepped up, and the boys mocked him. Daniel, filled with confidence in his friend, encouraged Max to show them his speed.

"Ready? Set. Go!" Daniel shouted as he stood at the race's starting line.

The kids took off running, and Max demonstrated his incredible speed. The spectators were amazed, and the bullies had to catch their breath after the race.

Daniel ran over to Max and gave him a high-five. "You should try out for the track team next year!" he suggested.

One of the bullies, named Chris, approached Max and said, "We're sorry for making fun of you."

Max nodded and looked at Daniel with a smile. "I think we shouldn't treat anyone differently. We all have our strengths."

"You're right," Chris agreed. "Thank you for racing with us. It was a lot of fun."

As they all ran off to race again together, Daniel knew that Max's kindness and acceptance had left a lasting impact on their classmates. He realized that judging people based on appearances was a mistake, and he made a mental note to always treat others with kindness, just as Max did.

Courage on the Court

Have you ever been passionate about something you wanted to pursue, even if it meant stepping out of your comfort zone? Did you feel a surge of nervousness when you were about to start? Well, you're not alone. It's perfectly normal to feel jittery when trying something new.

The good news is that, despite the fear, you can push through and do what you love, and that fear will eventually fade away.

Meet Ethan, a young boy who had a deep passion for playing basketball. He loved shooting hoops in his driveway, but he'd never joined a basketball team because he was too shy around others. One day, he decided to ask his dad if he could sign up for a basketball team. The thought of playing with a team, learning new skills, and competing in real games excited him.

In the weeks leading up to the team's first practice, Ethan could be found practicing his dribbling, shooting, and passing skills every day. But as the first practice approached, he began to feel more and more nervous. A few days before his first practice, his mom asked, "Are you excited about basketball practice?"

Ethan hesitated, feeling the nervousness creeping in. "Not really," he admitted. "I'm scared. I don't think I want to join the team anymore."

His mom nodded understandingly. "Is it because you're shy around new people?"

Ethan nodded. He was fine playing basketball by himself, but the idea of playing with a team and in front of others made him anxious.

His dad sat down beside him, placing a reassuring hand on his shoulder. "Ethan, it's completely normal to feel nervous when you're trying something new. But remember, that nervousness will fade once you get out there and start playing with your teammates."

Ethan took a deep breath and considered his dad's words. They made sense, and his dad was usually right about these things. He decided to give it a try. For a while, he felt better about the idea.

However, the night before his first practice, Ethan lay in bed, unable to sleep. Thoughts raced through his mind. What if he couldn't keep up with the other players?

What if he made mistakes and let the team down? What if he accidentally scored in the wrong hoop? His stomach churned with anxiety, and he began to doubt his decision.

The next morning, as he sat down for breakfast, Ethan made a tough decision. "Mom, Dad," he said, "I don't think I'm going to basketball practice today. I'm too nervous and scared."

Although it was hard for him to admit, Ethan felt a sense of relief. He didn't want to face the anxiety of playing in front of others.

His dad, sensing his inner turmoil, sat down beside him and said, "Ethan, I understand that you're nervous, but let me share a little secret with you. Everyone gets nervous before trying something new. Every single person. And if you're not nervous, it means it might not be that important to you. But once you face your fear and give it a shot, that nervousness will start to fade away."

Listening to his dad's words, Ethan began to realize that his fear was a natural part of trying something new. There had been other times when he felt nervous at first, but once he took the leap, the butterflies in his stomach disappeared.

"Okay, Dad," Ethan said with determination. "I'll do it!"

When Ethan arrived at practice that day, he saw a group of boys huddled together, looking just as nervous as he felt. He remembered what his dad had said about trying something new, so he mustered up the courage to approach the group and said, "Hey, guys! I'm Ethan. What are your names?"

Soon, they were all chatting, laughing, and getting to know each other. When the coaches arrived, Ethan was surprised to see his dad among them. His dad had volunteered to help the coaches, hoping it would ease Ethan's nerves.

As the practice sessions continued, Ethan discovered that he was just as skilled as his teammates, and he even taught them some new basketball tricks. It was a lot of fun, and he felt more comfortable with each practice.

The day of the first game arrived, and with it came a fresh wave of nervousness for Ethan. However, he was determined not to let his fear hold him back. He closed his eyes, took a deep breath, and remembered his dad's words about everyone feeling nervous when trying something new. With newfound courage, Ethan opened his eyes and stepped onto the basketball court.

When the game began, he chased after the ball, dribbled down the court, and made a fantastic shot. It sailed through the hoop, and Ethan couldn't contain his excitement. He had scored his first basket! He felt a surge of happiness, knowing that facing his fear had been worth it.

The Power of Being You

Do you ever think about how people see you? Do you worry about how you look or what clothes you wear? Well, you don't need to at all. No matter how you look, what style your hair is, how you dress, or what shoes you wear,

You are unique and special on the inside just as much as the outside.

Meet Alex, a boy with a mop of wild, curly hair. If you've ever seen a field of wheat blowing in the wind, you'd get the idea of the texture of Alex's hair. Alex loved to experiment with his unruly hair, and his wild curls provided endless opportunities for creativity. Each day, he'd try something new – one day, he'd slick it back; the next, he'd let it go wild and untamed. His hair was his canvas, and he was the artist.

As he strolled through the school corridors, it was a daily ritual for someone to comment, "Hey, Alex! Your hair looks awesome today!" These compliments brought a smile to his face, and he cherished the attention his hair garnered.

Alex found joy in the endless possibilities his hair offered and cherished the time spent with his mom before bed, scouring the internet for new hairstyles to try the next day.

In addition to his passion for hair, Alex relished spending time with his younger brother, Ben. They shared a close bond, often cycling through the neighborhood, creating intricate chalk patterns for games of hopscotch and four-square.

Today, they were returning from the park, with Alex cracking jokes, trying to get Ben to laugh uproariously.

Suddenly, Ben laughed so hard that he lost his footing. His laughter turned into a surprised yelp as he fell forward, landing on his knees. Concerned, Alex rushed to his side. Ben was picking himself up when Alex noticed a scrape on his knee. It looked a bit bloody but not too severe. "We should clean this up," Alex suggested, guiding his brother indoors.

After tending to Ben's scraped knee, Alex breathed a sigh of relief. But as he turned to leave the bathroom, his mom said, "Alex, what's in your hair?" Alex instinctively ran his fingers through his curls and felt something sticky,

Turning toward the mirror, he exclaimed, "Oh, no!" It was a large, sticky wad of bubble gum lodged in his hair, collecting more strands as he attempted to remove it.

"Alex, honey," his mom said, gently taking his hand, "the more you try to remove it, the worse it might get."

"I'm sorry, Alex," Ben chimed in. "I think I spit my gum out when I fell."

Alex looked at his younger brother, wanting to ease his guilt. He knew it was an accident, and Ben wouldn't intentionally do something like this. "Thank you, Ben," Alex replied, giving him a quick hug. "Mom can help me get it out."

Despite their attempts with ice, peanut butter, cooking oil, and vinegar, nothing worked to remove the gum from Alex's hair. After a while, his mom said, "I'm sorry, sweetie. I think we'll have to go to the hairdresser."

"What does that mean?" Alex asked, feeling a sense of dread.

"It means we'll have to cut the gum out, but remember, hair grows continuously, so it'll grow back," his mom assured him.

With a heavy heart, Alex agreed, worrying about how he would be perceived after getting his hair cut. He cherished his wild curls and wondered if people would still know him or like him the same way.

"Okay, Mom," Alex said with a small voice.

His mom hugged him tightly. "It's going to be okay, I promise. Think of it as a new style."

"Okay," Alex replied hesitantly. "But what if no one likes my new hair? What do I do then?"

"Alex, you're an amazing boy with so many talents. You're smart, funny, and have a kind heart. Everyone will love your hair, and they'll like you just as much as they did yesterday."

Feeling somewhat reassured, Alex joined his mom on a trip to the beauty salon. Climbing into the chair, he expressed his nervousness to the hairdresser, who smiled and said, "That's completely normal. We all get a little nervous when trying something new. I'll make sure your hair looks amazing, okay?"

Alex felt a bit more at ease after sharing his feelings. He closed his eyes as the hairdresser began to work, feeling the snip, snip, snip of his long, gummed-up curls falling to the floor. After a few moments, he opened his eyes to see his new hairstyle – shorter but still uniquely his.

His mom came over with a smile and said, "Look! I found some great hairstyles for shorter hair."

The next morning, Alex and his mom adorned his hair with new hair accessories, pulling back the sides. As he climbed the bus stairs, he tried not to make eye contact with the bus driver, feeling a bit self-conscious.

However, the bus driver surprised him, saying, "Hey! You changed your hair!" Alex nodded nervously.

"It looks great! It's a nice change!" the bus driver exclaimed, closing the door.

Alex felt a wave of relief wash over him, grateful for the kind words from the bus driver. And he realized that the bus driver's compliment wasn't an isolated incident.

Throughout the day, people he didn't even know yet praised his new hairstyle. By the end of the day, Alex concluded that the accidental gum incident had led him to embrace a change that was, in the end, quite refreshing.

So, what do you think of Alex's story? Just like Alex learned that no matter what you look like on the outside, your inner qualities remain unchanged. And if you ever find gum stuck in your hair, remember, there's always a way to fix it! Don't be afraid to embrace your uniqueness; your differences are what make you special and extraordinary.

Hey There

Thank you for reaching this point in the book!

I thoroughly enjoyed writing this chapter and sincerely hope you found it beneficial. If you have a moment, I would greatly appreciate hearing your thoughts on how you've enjoyed the book thus far.

Your honest feedback means the world to me and is invaluable in helping me improve my future content and create the best resources possible.

You can share your thoughts by visiting the following link or scanning the provided QR code.

SCAN THE QR CODE OR VISIT:

www.bit.ly/inspiringboy

Thank you for taking the time to leave your feedback. Now let's get back into the book.

Dive Beyond Fear

Alex had always been drawn to the mysterious depths of the ocean. The thought of exploring the underwater world, with its vibrant coral reefs and enchanting marine life, filled his dreams.

He longed to become a certified scuba diver so he could finally immerse himself in the wonders beneath the surface.

His opportunity came one sunny morning when he signed up for scuba diving lessons. The excitement bubbled inside him as he listened to his instructor explain the basics of diving, from equipment to safety procedures. Alex knew this was the first step toward fulfilling his lifelong dream.

The journey into the world of scuba diving wasn't without its challenges. The gear felt cumbersome at first, making Alex feel like a clumsy astronaut on Earth. But he persisted, knowing that mastering these tools was essential to his underwater adventures.

During one of his early training dives, panic gripped him as he watched his air gauge dip into the red zone. His heart raced, and a wave of fear threatened to engulf him.

But he remembered his instructor's advice: "Stay calm and follow the procedures." With measured breaths, he signaled to his buddy, who shared some air. Together, they ascended safely to the surface. It was a terrifying experience, but it taught Alex a valuable lesson about keeping his composure in the face of fear.

As weeks turned into months, Alex became more proficient in diving. His skills improved, and his confidence grew. Each dive brought new discoveries and breathtaking sights, from encountering a playful school of fish to witnessing a graceful sea turtle glide by. These experiences only deepened his passion for the ocean.

The day finally arrived when Alex was scheduled for his final certification dive. He couldn't help but feel a mixture of excitement and trepidation.

His mom, who had always supported his dreams, asked the instructor, "How long until he can go on his own diving adventures?

He's been looking forward to this for so long."

The instructor, an experienced diver with a weathered face and a twinkle in his eye, considered the question. "He should wait a few more days to build confidence," he advised. "Once he feels more at ease, he can start with easy dives. Scuba diving is a fantastic experience, but it's important to take it one step at a time."

Alex took a deep breath and awaited the instructor's guidance. "Okay," he said with determination. "I'll be careful, and I'll follow the rules."

At home, Alex found himself hesitating to approach his scuba gear. The fear of making a mistake, of not being skilled enough, lingered in the back of his mind. His mom, perceptive as always, noticed his reluctance and decided it was time for a heart-to-heart conversation.

"Alex, let's talk," his mom said one evening as they sat on the porch, the setting sun casting a warm glow around them. Alex wondered if he was in trouble, his heart racing with anxiety. His mom smiled gently, sensing his concern. "No, you're not in trouble," she reassured him. "I want to understand why you're avoiding diving."

Alex bit his lip, struggling to admit his fear. He had always seen himself as brave, but this vulnerability was unfamiliar territory. Finally, with a quiver in his voice, he confessed, "I'm scared, Mom."

His mom wrapped her arms around him, providing a comforting embrace. "It's okay to be afraid, sweetheart," she whispered. "But remember, you've trained hard for this, and you love scuba diving. Don't let fear stand in your way."

Alex nodded, tears glistening in his eyes. His mom's words offered solace, and he realized that speaking his fear out loud made it feel less overwhelming. Maybe, he thought, opening up about his feelings wasn't a sign of weakness but a source of strength.

"Would you like to give it a try tomorrow?" his mom asked. "I'll be there to support you, and you can start with an easy dive, just like the instructor suggested."

Alex wiped away his tears, summoned a shaky smile, and nodded. "Yes," he said, determination glinting in his eyes. He was still afraid, but he knew he couldn't let fear rob him of his passion.

The following morning, Alex found himself standing at the edge of the ocean, his heart racing with a heady mix of anticipation and fear. The waves lapped gently at the shore, as if encouraging him to take the plunge. He glanced at his mom, who stood beside him, her presence reassuring.

He picked up his scuba gear, each piece now a familiar friend.

As he donned the wetsuit, strapped on the tank, and checked his equipment meticulously, he felt a sense of purpose wash over him. The fear was there, lurking in the background, but he was determined not to let it control him.

With his gear in place, he waded into the water, feeling the gradual shift from solid ground to the weightless buoyancy of the ocean. The moment he descended beneath the surface, he was enveloped in a world of breathtaking beauty. Vibrant coral formations stretched out before him, teeming with an array of colorful fish.

As he explored the underwater realm, his initial apprehension gave way to a sense of wonder and exhilaration. He marveled at the intricate dance of a clownfish, the graceful movements of a manta ray, and the ethereal beauty of a coral garden. His heart swelled with gratitude for the opportunity to witness this hidden world.

When he finally resurfaced, a radiant smile adorned his face, and his eyes sparkled with joy.

He realized that he had conquered his fear, not by ignoring it, but by confronting it head-on. Fear had been a formidable adversary, but his passion for scuba diving had proven to be an even stronger force.

As he swam back to the shore, his mom waiting with open arms, he couldn't help but feel a profound sense of accomplishment. He had faced his fear, and in doing so, he had unlocked a world of endless possibilities.

Alex learned that day that fear should never be an insurmountable barrier. It was a natural emotion, a reminder that he was embarking on something meaningful and challenging. But it was a feeling he could acknowledge and then set aside to make room for his dreams.

So, if Alex could conquer his fear, you can too. Don't let fear hold you back from doing what you love and achieving your dreams. Remember, you are unique, and you deserve to chase after everything you desire with unwavering determination.

Wings of Appreciation

Have you ever had someone special in your life who's always there for you? Someone you go to when you need help or when things are tough? Well, just like you have good days and bad days, so do they. Sometimes, the people we love need our help and support too.

This story is about a special boy who does something nice for someone he cares about when they're feeling sad.

Owen and his grandfather sat in the backyard, working on a treehouse they had been building together. They were very focused, and while Owen couldn't look at his grandpa because he knew they would start laughing together, even though they were in a serious moment, he knew that his grandpa's brow was furrowed in concentration.

Grandpa hammered the last nail into the treehouse platform, securing it in place. He wiped the sweat from his brow and turned to look at Owen, grinning. "Ah, grandson, we've finished it!"

Owen jumped up, excited, and they did their "finishing dance" together, a silly little jig they had made up. "Come on," Grandpa said, ruffling Owen's hair. "Let's go inside for some cookies and milk."

Owen loved spending time with his grandpa, whether it was building treehouses, fishing, or just telling stories. They had been doing these same things for years. Owen's grandpa was a retired carpenter, and his favorite thing was building things with Owen. Owen had been helping him since he could hold a hammer, and even before that, he would watch his grandpa work from his playpen. Their special traditions always brought joy and warmth to their hearts.

One day, Owen had a rough day at school. He got a poor grade on a test he thought he would ace, and it put him in a sour mood for the rest of the day. Little things seemed to irritate him, and he found himself feeling frustrated. At lunch, he accidentally knocked over his tray, spilling food everywhere, and his classmates teased him mercilessly. When he got home, he went straight to his room, not even acknowledging his dad's greeting.

Later, Owen heard a soft knock on his bedroom door. "Hello, Owen," Grandpa's warm voice greeted him as he entered the room.

"Your dad told me you had a tough day, and I wanted to see if I could help."

Owen didn't know what would make him feel better, so he shrugged. Just knowing that Grandpa cared made him feel a little lighter.

Grandpa put his arm around Owen, and they sat together on the bed. Owen started talking about his bad day, showing his scraped finger and recounting the lunchroom teasing. As he spoke, his voice wavered, but he felt stronger with Grandpa by his side, just listening.

"Everyone has bad days and meets people who try to make them feel bad about themselves," Grandpa said, placing a hand on Owen's heart. "It's how you choose to react that defines you. If you hold onto those bad feelings, you're choosing to stay uncomfortable. But if you let go and understand that those people are unhappy too, you'll find peace."

Owen listened to his wise grandpa and nodded. He decided to let go of the bad feelings, closing his eyes to feel better.

"Good," Grandpa said, encouraging him. "Now, replace the bad feelings with good ones. Tell me one good thing about today."

Owen opened his eyes and smiled. "You came to see me and make me feel better!"

Grandpa laughed. "That's a great feeling! I'm happy to see you too!"

As they sat together, Owen felt the warmth of his grandpa's support and love. That evening, after dinner, Owen said to his dad, "Grandpa always helps me. I wish I could do something special for him to thank him for everything."

"What do you want to do?" his dad asked.

"I think I want to build him something special," Owen replied. "A model airplane, maybe."

"Then let's do it," his dad said. "I'll help you get the supplies, but you can build it yourself."

With his dad's support, Owen worked on the model airplane every day after school. He remembered the skills his grandpa had taught him, and it didn't take long to assemble the model. Owen painted it with care and named it "Grandpa's Pride."

When Owen presented the model airplane to his grandpa, he was thrilled. "Thank you for this wonderful gift, Owen!" Grandpa exclaimed. "It's the best model airplane I've ever seen."

Owen smiled. "Thank you for being an amazing grandpa. I love you so much."

They shared a heartfelt hug, and then Owen, his dad, and Grandpa took the model airplane out for its maiden flight, created with love and gratitude by Owen himself.

Oliver's Tasty Adventure

Oliver was a boy with a heart full of curiosity. He had an insatiable appetite for trying new things, and his boundless enthusiasm made him known as "Oliver the Adventurous" among his friends and family.

From a young age, he had been drawn to a wide array of hobbies and activities. Whether it was painting landscapes, hiking through the woods, tinkering with old radios, or attempting to bake intricate desserts, Oliver put his heart and soul into every endeavor.

As he grew older, Oliver couldn't help but notice that many people around him had discovered their true passions. His older sister, Emma, was an accomplished violinist, and his best friend, Leo, had an undeniable talent for coding and technology. Even his parents, both successful doctors, were deeply committed to their work. It seemed as though everyone had their "thing," their calling, something that ignited their souls.

One day, Oliver decided it was time to embark on a quest of his own—a journey to uncover his true passion. He started by making a list of all the activities he had ever tried and enjoyed Painting, hiking, radio repair, and baking were at the top of the list, but none of them felt like the one thing he wanted to dedicate his life to.

With a determination in his heart, Oliver began to explore each of his interests more deeply. He spent hours in the forest near his home, learning about the flora and fauna. He studied the works of famous painters, experimented with different artistic styles, and even held a small art exhibition at his school. While he loved art, it didn't quite capture his heart as the one true passion he sought.

Next, Oliver delved into the world of electronics and radio repair. He spent countless evenings disassembling old radios, soldering wires, and studying circuits. It was fascinating, and he felt a sense of accomplishment with each successfully restored device. Yet, despite his growing expertise, he knew it wasn't the single passion he was searching for.

Baking came next on his journey of exploration. Oliver enrolled in baking classes,

Baking brought him joy, and he enjoyed sharing his creations with friends and family, but something still felt missing.

One evening, as Oliver was reflecting on his quest, he had an idea. He decided to seek advice from those who had already found their passions. He reached out to his sister, Emma, and asked her how she had discovered her love for the violin.

Emma smiled warmly at her brother. "Oliver, it wasn't always the violin for me," she confessed. "I explored various instruments and forms of art before I found my true passion. It was a journey of self-discovery. The violin simply resonated with me on a deep level, and I knew it was what I wanted to pursue."

Encouraged by Emma's words, Oliver sought guidance from his friend Leo, who was a coding prodigy. Leo shared his own story of trial and error, explaining how he had dabbled in multiple tech-related hobbies before finding his calling in coding. "It's about following your

Oliver's quest continued. He expanded his list of activities to explore and joined a hiking club to deepen his connection with nature. He discovered the joy of navigating through the wilderness, observing wildlife, and embracing the serenity of the great outdoors. While hiking brought him immense happiness, it still didn't feel like the singular passion he sought.

One day, while baking in the kitchen, Oliver had an epiphany. He realized that the joy he found in baking was not just about creating delicious treats; it was about the science and artistry behind it. He loved experimenting with ingredients, understanding the chemical reactions, and crafting intricate designs. It was the combination of creativity and precision that made his heart sing.

With newfound clarity, Oliver decided to explore the world of culinary arts further. He enrolled in culinary school, where he immersed himself in the complexities of cooking and baking. He learned from accomplished chefs and honed his skills in the kitchen. Oliver was enthralled by the fusion of art and science in culinary arts, and he knew he had found his true passion.

Years passed, and Oliver became a renowned chef known for his innovative dishes and artistic presentations. He opened his own restaurant, where he could express his culinary creativity to the fullest. His journey of self-discovery had led him to a place where his heart was truly content.

Oliver's story served as an inspiration to many, reminding them that the path to discovering one's passion was often a winding one. It required curiosity, exploration, and the willingness to learn from each experience. Just like Oliver, they too could find their true calling by following their hearts and embracing the journey of self-discovery.

In the end, Oliver's adventurous spirit had led him to the most fulfilling destination of all: the discovery of his passion and the realization that it was a journey well worth taking. His experiences had taught him that the pursuit of one's true calling was not a race but a deeply personal voyage.

And so, just like Oliver, remember that your "thing" may take time to discover. Embrace your curiosity, explore new horizons, and trust that your passion will find you.

A Symphony of Stars

In the quiet, rural town of Willowbrook, the nights were as still as the depths of space. Nestled among rolling hills and fields, the town was far from the city lights, making it a perfect spot for stargazers.

Among the residents was a young boy named Noah, whose fascination with the cosmos knew no bounds.

Noah had always been an explorer at heart. His eyes sparkled with curiosity as he looked up at the night sky, marveling at the vast expanse of stars that stretched out above him. Unlike his peers, who were more interested in video games and sports, Noah's passion lay in the mysteries of the universe.

One evening, as he lay on a blanket in his backyard, Noah spotted a shooting star streaking across the sky. With a heart full of wonder, he made a silent wish upon that celestial visitor. "I wish I could share my love for the stars with others," he whispered.

The next day at school, Noah couldn't contain his excitement. He told his classmates about the shooting star and how he wished to share the beauty of the night sky with them.

While some kids seemed interested, others shrugged it off, dismissing it as just another one of Noah's peculiar interests.

Undeterred, Noah decided to take matters into his own hands. He asked his parents for a telescope, and with their support, he purchased a small one that he could afford with his allowance. He spent countless nights on his roof, observing planets, galaxies, and constellations, all while taking notes and sketching what he saw.

His dedication soon caught the attention of a few classmates who were willing to give stargazing a chance. Noah eagerly invited them over for a stargazing night at his house. Armed with the telescope and his growing knowledge of the night sky, he guided his friends through the cosmos.

Their initial skepticism turned into amazement as they gazed upon Jupiter's mighty bands and the delicate beauty of the Orion Nebula.

Word of Noah's stargazing nights spread through the school, and more and more students became intrigued by the idea of exploring the universe. Noah was ecstatic. He created a stargazing club, and its membership quickly grew. Meetings were held on clear nights, and the group would gather on the school's rooftop, their eyes fixed on the heavens.

One evening, as they observed a meteor shower, Noah overheard a conversation among his classmates. They were talking about how their shared passion for stargazing had brought them closer together. A sense of pride and fulfillment washed over him. His wish had come true. He was sharing his love for the stars with others, and in doing so, he had forged new friendships.

The stargazing club became more than just a hobby; it was a tight-knit community bound by wonder and curiosity. Noah's leadership and enthusiasm were infectious, and he inspired his peers to embrace their own interests, no matter how unique they seemed.

As the months passed, the stargazing club decided to organize a community stargazing event, open to everyone in Willowbrook. They contacted local astronomers, borrowed larger telescopes, and prepared a presentation about the night sky. The event was a resounding success, drawing families from all over town. People marveled at the celestial wonders that had always been there but had often gone unnoticed.

One clear night, as Noah lay on his blanket, gazing up at the stars, he couldn't help but smile. The once-quiet town of Willowbrook had transformed into a place where the night sky was celebrated and appreciated. And it all started with his simple wish upon a shooting star.

As graduation approached, Noah knew that he was leaving behind a legacy of curiosity and unity in Willowbrook. He had shown his community the beauty of the universe and the power of shared passions.

Noah's story reminded everyone that it was okay to be different, to have unique interests, and to chase their dreams. It was a reminder that, just like the stars in the night sky, we all have something special to offer, and when we share it with others, we create connections that can light up the world.

The Pumpkin King

Have you ever been passionate about something but faced obstacles and setbacks that made you want to give up? That's exactly what happened to our young hero, Mason. He had a dream of growing the biggest pumpkin in his neighborhood for the annual pumpkin competition,

Mason had always been fascinated by gardening, and pumpkins, in particular, captured his imagination. He spent hours researching and reading about pumpkin cultivation. One day, he decided it was time to turn his dream into reality. With determination burning in his heart, he approached his dad for some advice. His dad, a seasoned gardener, shared a wealth of pumpkin-growing wisdom and gave him a packet of special pumpkin seeds.

"Thanks, Dad, but I want to do this on my own," Mason said with enthusiasm. His dad smiled, patted him on the back, and said, "You've got this, Mason. Remember, it's okay to ask for help if you need it."

Mason set off to start his pumpkin-growing journey. He carefully chose a sunny spot in their backyard, cleared the soil of weeds, and prepared it with nutrient-rich compost. His hands, once clean, now bore the brown earthy stains of hard work, and he couldn't have been happier.

With great care, he planted the pumpkin seeds in neat rows, each one placed at the perfect depth. Every morning, Mason would rush to the garden, eager to see signs of life emerging from the soil. It was a waiting game, but his patience was rewarded when tiny green shoots finally pushed through the earth.

Weeks passed, and Mason watched his pumpkin plants grow taller and healthier. He even gave them names – Peter, Paul, and Percy. Every evening, he would spend hours tending to them, watering them gently, and singing songs to them. Mason was on cloud nine.

One sunny morning, Mason noticed something peculiar – Peter's leaves were turning yellow. Fear gripped him as he examined the sickly plant. Panicked, he rushed to consult his gardening books but couldn't find any answers. He decided to wait it out, hoping for the best.

Days turned into weeks, and Mason's precious pumpkins seemed to be withering away.

He couldn't sleep at night, worried about his beloved plants. Finally, he approached his dad and confessed, "Dad, I need your help. My pumpkins are dying, and I don't know what to do."

His dad nodded knowingly, and together, they examined the plants. Mason's dad identified a common pumpkin disease and showed him how to treat it. They sprayed a natural remedy, and Mason listened intently, soaking up the wisdom his father offered. Mason learned a valuable lesson that day – it's okay to seek help when you're facing a challenge, especially from those who have experience.

With newfound knowledge, Mason nursed his pumpkins back to health. They thrived under his care, and Mason's excitement grew as he watched them grow bigger each day. He marveled at how resilient his plants were, much like himself. The day of the pumpkin competition arrived, and Mason proudly carried his enormous pumpkin to the contest.

The competition was fierce, with giant pumpkins of all shapes and sizes on display. Mason's heart raced as he watched the judges inspect his pumpkin, measuring it meticulously. When they finally announced the winner, Mason's heart soared. His pumpkin was the biggest and the most beautiful. He had done it!

Mason realized that while his journey had been filled with ups and downs, he had learned and grown so much from the experience. It wasn't just about winning; it was about pursuing his passion and never giving up, even when faced with adversity.

And so, Mason continued his gardening adventures, knowing that each challenge was an opportunity to learn and grow, just like his magnificent pumpkin. He spent countless hours in the garden, nurturing not just pumpkins but also a deep love for nature and resilience in the face of obstacles.

As the years went by, Mason became known in the neighborhood as the "Pumpkin King," a title he wore with pride.

He shared his gardening wisdom with others, helping them overcome challenges and grow beautiful pumpkins of their own. Mason's garden became a place of learning and community, where friends and neighbors gathered to celebrate their shared love for gardening.

And every fall, Mason's giant pumpkins stood proudly in the annual competition, a testament to the power of determination, perseverance, and the joy of pursuing one's passion.

In the end, Mason understood that life, like gardening, was a journey of growth and discovery. He had learned that setbacks were just stepping stones on the path to success, and that the sweetest victories were often born from the toughest challenges.

Epilogue

Now that you've heard the stories of these amazing boys and the hurdles they've conquered, remember that you can do it too. You are an exceptional boy, and there is no one else in the world quite like you. Whenever you face fear, uncertainty, or doubt, take a deep breath and keep pushing forward. This is how you'll achieve remarkable things in the world.

Remember that it's okay to make mistakes; they are stepping stones on your journey to success. Learn from them and use them as opportunities to grow stronger and wiser. Surround yourself with positive influences and supportive friends who uplift and inspire you.

Believe in yourself, even when others may doubt you. Your potential is limitless, and your future is full of endless possibilities. With determination, resilience, and a positive attitude, you can overcome any obstacle and achieve greatness. Keep your head held high, young man, for you are destined for incredible things."